WHERE GOOD SWIMMERS DROWN

WHERE GOOD SWIMMERS DROWN

Susan Elbe

Concrete Wolf
Poetry Chapbook Series

Copyright 2012 Susan Elbe

ISBN 978-0-9797137-6-7

Design: Tonya Namura

Cover art: Night Tide by Eric Zener

Author photo: Katrin Talbot

Concrete Wolf Poetry Chapbook Series

Concrete Wolf
PO Box 1808
Kingston, WA 98346

http://ConcreteWolf.com

ConcreteWolf@yahoo.com

Acknowledgments

Grateful acknowledgment to the editors of the following publications where these poems first appeared, sometimes in different form:

diode (online): "How to Fall," "Where Good Swimmers Drown," "Lunar," "The End of Love," "Once Not, Now Broken," *"What he kissed in me"*

LOCUSPOINT (online): "Virgo"

OCHO: "About the House"

The Poetry Center of Chicago 14th Juried Reading—Third Place (online): "Putting Love in Its Place"

qarrtsiluni: "Neon in a Jar"

The Rondeau Roundup (blog): "My, What Big Wishes I Had." Reprinted in The Writer Magazine (October 2011)

Salt Hill: "Not Quite Love"

"Where Good Swimmers Drown" is also the winner of the 7th Annual Oneiros Press Broadside Competition. "Not Quite Love" also appeared on limited edition postcards designed and distributed by Poetry Jumps Off the Shelf.

Table of Contents

Where Good Swimmers Drown	3
How to Fall	4
New Flowers Opening	6
Putting Love in Its Place	7
My, What Big Wishes I Had	9
Dead-Eye Moth	10
At Black Canyon	11
How We Are American	12
Virgo	13
Not Quite Love	15
What he kissed in me	16
Neon in a Jar	18
The Hazards of Magic	19
Instinctive Drowning Response	21
In the Stunned Light of October	22
Goodbye Starts Something Like This	23
The End of Love	24
All Night the Snow	25
About the House	26
Lunar	27
Simple Erotics	28
Horses in Virginia in November	30
The Deep Possible	32
Once Not, Now Broken	33
Notes	35
About the Author	37

Where Good Swimmers Drown

Where Good Swimmers Drown

In small towns with one undertaker,
a grocer, six taverns,
and bottomless backwoods lakes,
where my five-and-dime locket sinks
down and down,
disappearing like a silver minnow,
and my red sandals too,
small as doll shoes,
smaller as I float farther out.

I don't know what's underneath
but I know how
fast, fast cars can fly, the souls
of farm boys getting trapped in bottles,
and god knows it feels good,
the wind picking up,
soft weeds braceleting my wrists,
the shoreline curved
into a smile I can remember, just.

How to Fall

Start by leaving home. It's not where the heart is,
but where the hard edge is. When ice begins
to ebb from shore freeing mangy marsh grass,
leave.

And as you pick up speed, let your life arc out,
away from you.

Realize you don't know where you're going
and the weather changes often.
Steer between the stars
like songbirds coming back at night.
Listen to the whirring
of a thousand, thousand miles of dark.

Remember you are ancient,
that once you walked out of the sea
and in the trees became another thing.
Know you can again.

Become three kinds of lonely.

Light a torch.
Leave a trail of handprints on the walls.

Or start by staying put. Sit
underneath the porch light. Eat walnuts
and persimmons. Spread your red-edged wings.
"Calling time" begins near midnight.

Be a whisper looking for a mouth:
luna, luna, luna.

Be hungry. Want.

Women are locks. Men open them for doors.

New Flowers Opening

Spring came on that year snowing magnolias.
We drove out past the city limits.
You had your brights on
but we never found our way.
After that, dirt roads and shady turn-offs,
the larded light of small, exhausted towns
glowing in the distance. Arrival,
far. A sloped horizon, farther still.
The detours made me strong.

Putting Love in Its Place

This is how we lay down love,
in the chain-smoking dark
a glow that eats itself to ash.

This is where we lay it down.
Underneath,
where what we lose, finds us.

Once we were an all-night city,
the moon-skinned clouds
the mole-blind river.

We stepped into the water
and became the boat,
a shimmer in the upside-down.

On a park bench, we forgot
our lives and let them
come to us, wind-smacked,

crumpled, the cheap ink
of romance staining us,
a mystery of misinformation.

This is why we lay down love,
because all there is is
wreckage we return to,

a dim-lamped room
of memory, its flimsy curtains
blowing summer in,

large between us, the unrumpled bed,
a hard pine in our throats.
This is how we lay down, love,

in the slattern, kissing dark,
in the unmasked part,
in the kicking-can emptiness
of the unasked-for heart.

My, What Big Wishes I Had

I could not calculate my nature then,
too stunned by street and kitchen din.
Oh, the summer city bruised but did not
burn me, the night's load of slushy heat caught
by sooty screens that let no breezes in.

That was before your autumn weather's spin
undid me, its blue, lake-bitten wind,
chrome-dented light, and all its heart-cold plot.
I could not calculate my nature then.

No taffeta and locket, my old friend,
no sweet and butter-crumble, no bride, when
I thought nothing mattered but a love knot.
Loving you was always the long-shot,
a blind bet, underlay, the dividend
              I could not calculate.

Dead-Eye Moth

Iris rust and yellow jackets tango in the eaves,
                    hunting windless homes.

Summer's crude seams pull apart,
life straining at its flimsy clothes.

A lone moth begins its Braille, reading rift and dip
along the mildewed walls.

Geese too begin aligning wings to the weight
                    of salt and distance.

Today again, I loved imperfectly and too well,
failed in what comes easily to others,

the once-wild moth in me
rising to the point of only ample music—

remembered snippets,
                    not the whole score.

I'll wake tomorrow to what I knew I'd be,
                    ghost peddler,

haunted and between loves,
shadows clinging to my hands, their smell
                    of root and mud,

everywhere
          the furred,
                    incessant green.

AT BLACK CANYON

In the snapshots I found, you lean
over that dark sluice of stone
split with a ribbon of light,
the tattooed birds on your shoulders
leaning and leaning
until I thought they would fly.
When I let you hold me at the hips
and bend me to that darkness too,
I felt safe as I did as a child
breathing deep in the closet
among woolen hems and feather ticking,
savoring the musky scent of life.

But all night in our gauzy tent of stars,
I listened to your breath
in sleep, rising up
from deeper than the river
gasping far below us,
measured as the pulse of cold
steel you insisted on beneath your pillow,
the blue wings folded over
your heart, everything
locked down tight against
the untamable calling out to us,
that salvation nothing you could use.

How We Are American

You carry Kansas under your tongue like a dry creek
and your eyes hold the persistent, see-through
light of wind-gnawed fields.
When you open your hand, the sky turns
black with wings.

When I uncurl my fist, there's a city in my palm,
backyards deepening to blue, cold
stars spilling over wash lines,
the dark streets of girlhood. My heart, ragged
skyline, no horizon.

You keep saving all your dreams for the rainy day
you can't see is here. I'm the lottery
I hope you'll keep trying,
though the odds are huge. We're always
wanting to make sense of us,

our need to be alone but surrounded by the world,
constantly surviving some useless war,
wanting to believe again,
needing love to be larger than life, drive-up,
drive-through, drive-in.

Sometimes I wonder if this freedom's worth it.
Too many times we've been like this—
proud and yearning, divided
and star-spangled, our bodies in the dark,
waiting for fireworks to begin.

Virgo

You think "earth" but I am river-fed,
a lake silted and flayed
by the moon,

its tin-bitter light smearing me blue
with the junk of metaphor.
Blinkered and blinking

on the ceiling of night, I'm an electric
angel, wrangling to break
through the swink and the sin.

You think "sheaves" but I am thistle,
my hair a dry lightning,
my feet planted deep.

I carry longing in a sling, the child
old enough to walk but won't.
It stoops my shoulders.

You think "shy" but I am harsh,
a wicked wind rattling
windows, howling

through the strange houses I dream
each night, everything lost
inside mutable mirrors.

You think "mercurial" but I am the steel
winter light that sticks
in your throat. I am orphan

and old country, fiddle-fish and wolf.
I am salt in the wound
that keeps opening.

Not Quite Love

Full of rankle and sweet talk,
I'm lately lovelorn
I'm lately so
full of candor and thorn.

Full of winter and brack talk,
You're lately shopworn
You're lately so
full of distance and mourn.

We can't decide how not to talk,
we're lately forsworn
we're lately so
riddled with crevice and scorn.

Full of wrangle and cheap talk,
I'm lately reborn
I'm lately so
shaken with shiver, and torn.

What he kissed in me

was the bear, the great bruin,
                               big-pawed ursa.

The bed was crowded.
The world was old.
We were young.
The bear slumbered.

It was winter and outside snow
                               flew against the windows,

white moths,
wet feathers,
slick comet lines.

He wanted me mythic and curled into the cave of him,
my claw and fang hooded in dream,
                               wanted me

drowsy and myopic.
But I did not go under,
never down
into the sockeye world.

No, I wanted the night sky, to lean against another
                               large-backed dark.

What he kissed in me
roused and reared up,
fiercely turning

to that flurry and beyond. Not sorry,
                    all night I outran him.

Neon in a Jar

> *based on Underwater C-Scape (Anemone), 2006, Pae White Electro-luminescent wire in a plastic container*

Buzzing at the glass, honey
with the sting still in,

a river's strong green, fire
following a tree-line,

blue prairie wind whistling through.
Kneeling inside, helpless

in the hands of good-time gods,
their hocus-pocus,

held rapt by this weather, we are lit
with lightning and no rain,

our eyes, the stubs of burnt-out stars,
no escape from our reflections.

The Hazards of Magic

The cripple of light opening against my back,
always the teeth of your words
                        sawing me in two.

Hitler said great liars are also great magicians
and so you were,
rowing me out as far as your arms
                            could pull us,

over into such bright rapids
                      they took my breath,

the power of such water, too much for me,
                    a white confusion.

I foundered though you said it wasn't deep,
and even when you opened
the false door, bringing us to shore,
                            I knew

we were trapped.

                            When night came on,

you said *look up*, and there,
                pulled from your sleeve

a whirl of bats, their wings a darker-than-night dark,
the sky, like you and I,

        shredding,

                shredding.

Instinctive Drowning Response

> *Except in rare circumstances, drowning people*
> *are physiologically unable to call out for help.*

I couldn't call for help.
Breath had to come first.

> *Nature instinctively forces the drowning*
> *to extend their arms laterally*
> *and press down on the water's surface.*

I couldn't wave for help,
the glyph of my arms

stretched across water,
pushing down to lift up

the sad oh of my mouth
sinking beneath.

> *From beginning to end drowning people's*
> *bodies remain upright in water,*
> *with no evidence of a supporting kick.*

I couldn't kick free
from the beautiful dark

of submersion, the hard
crucifixion of my own

stubborn belief.

In the Stunned Light of October

You knew I was never one of the crazy girls,
            but whatever you wanted,
                      I wanted it more.

    If this disappointment between us wasn't
            a border, river-wide,
                    barbed.

    If the days didn't go by unanswered, dead
            leaves scrattling down
                    sidewalks.

    If the stunned light wasn't faltering, if the sky
            was not basement-damp,
                    a frail tent.

    If the veiled moon didn't hang waterless,
            a chalky pill, while I am stuck
                    inside this rain.

    It's not the move, it's the nature of the move.
            If only you hadn't said
                    maybe.

Goodbye Starts Something Like This

A rough shurr beats against my sleep,
salt glazing, rotting everything.

Floors buckle and the light-blind
moth goes down.

In the gut, a rush of pleated silk
and I feel a distance settle

in the blue hollow of my throat.
A kill of splintered stars

washes up at my feet.
I bleed dark roses in the sand.

The End of Love

deep
among the flowers

back
to shadow

I tried,
but weary

this night I flew
and was left

All Night the Snow

You left like you always do
and December is a chain reaction
pileup on the interstate.

The sky, a dirty-white organdy pinafore,
swings slack and wet in the trees.

All night it snows.
All night the silence gathers in it.
All night the snow deepens.
All night the snow gathers in me.

Rabbits tremble underneath.
The furnace rests. Cold
flowers in the walls, electricity in the blankets.

Was it the palmist in Sausalito
or the Tarot reader in Chicago
who told me love was done this time around?

All night, the snow.
All night, this velvet pocket,
this mute tongue,
these slick cuffs of ice.
Even the crows, snugged and silent.

There are no edges until morning
when a snowplow scrapes away my sleep.

This living alone uses me in its way
but the light is slow, Lord,
the light is slow.

About the House

Some nights when I'm undone and naked
in my dreaming, the house gets up
and goes to you.

                Left unsheltered
in the middle of its absence
I wonder then if all the pieces fall
neatly into place or if each room gathers slowly.
I wonder if you've found the little girl
who used the drawers as ladder rungs
to reach the pantry shelves.

                On nights so cold
the window sashes crack and weep,
the house pulls hard toward you,
chuffing from its station, butter-yellow
windows smearing as it picks up speed.
I'm on the platform in my wind-swept skirt,
rust on my tongue.

You never understood how houses are like trains,
racing to us and away, sparks flying,
braking, breaking.

                Some nights when I want
to be a girl again, the house stays put
and you break in. I hear
the useless deadbolt's click, your footsteps
in the hall. I see the white moon
of your flashlight orbiting the rooms.
You steal nothing, yet everything is taken.

Lunar

Wasn't it lovely, under the New Flowers Opening
Moon, how I left the porch light on,
called you in, offered walnuts and persimmons?

And in the month of the Sunburn Moon,
that lunatic light tugging our tides, didn't we try,
really try to cool our hot heels in the dazzling lake?

That was the *two-fer* month when a Blue Moon
took us by surprise and we went deep into
the pond of our dreams, too deep to come up for air.

I forget. Did resistance start under the Sturgeon
Moon, steeped in green and the frantic buzz
of those who realize they won't live forever?

Or was it in the Moon of Spiderwebs on the Ground,
when a slow rot began in the trees, bruised
clouds gathering, the world leaning down on us?

No, it was in the Fall From Moon, that insane
bowed sky, the awful scrying stars. No dark side
but one we imagined. Christ, all those bladed blues.

Simple Erotics

something about September's ember
the bruised alcoves of clouds
and our wind-stuck mouths

something about the sad-elephant moon
and a stray edge of summer

you were the secret everyone knew but me

the fences blurred
the fields went fuzzy
I knew little about desire

you were my flight and my fall

I missed it in you then
but we were shy
so shy
like children in Sunday school photos

in every room we entered
the others were jealous

for a while a little while
I had the match that lit your wick

this is no souvenir elegy
no shopworn emotion

but a psalm to everything
young and new

oh you were a strange egg
deep excavation
steep stairway

I came to you like deer to salt lick

oh I would be like that again
oh

Horses in Virginia in November

                              Two horses stand

side-by-side this morning in the meadow,
all sad and shiny in a hard rain, the luminous

dark planets of their eyes reminding me
grief doesn't end, but comes and goes like weather,

like the moon, like your ghost that's found
and followed me, the way the Black is always
vigilant of the shy Bay.

                          They need each other

like I needed you, for history and for habit,
for heart. They stand with perfect attention

while freight trains rumble down the hollow
and day hauls its winter light over them.

Sometimes the shy Bay moves off from the Black,
wanting to feel his own power, ignoring
the other's plaintive come-near neigh.

But soon they come together again.

                            They need each other,

as touchstones, have settled between them what you
and I couldn't. Fenced by barbed wire, their lives

might seem poor and unvaried. But they have stars
the whirling stars at night and the stars

of halved apples held out in flat palms, sweet
clover littered with diamonds, the long-maned days.
This field is theirs,

                                      they have each other.

The Deep Possible

All the long Fall, I watched
the river, one day smoke with fog,
                the next with forming ice,
wafering out from shore, at first thin as mica,
                      then stepping deeper.

The trees burned briefly,
snuffed by cold's heavy fist,

and in the grip of this hard winter,
I forgot how to call life to me,
        to scoop a snowless circle in the yard,
scatter suet, crusty bread.

Dirty crags of snow along each curb,
streets glittering
           and bleached with salt.

Winter's weight hangs on, clenching me
              between its badger teeth,

the last days, haunted and thick with monotony.

I wait for the icy fist to open,
      for the river's warm breath to fog again,

for possibility to cast its spell,
chant its mantra in my blood,
              lay out its colored skirl of cards.

Once Not, Now Broken

Before you ask about my lightning mouth,
understand, I might have been a summer,
though I told like a hand,
though I told like a hammer.
and my demons never were ironic.

I was too possible, like death, like the world isn't.
Lethargic warrior, you didn't want an other,
you wanted a desert.

Before you ask about the love-struck bell,
think of all the stairs we had to climb,
the heaviness of iron, but how
once we got it going,
we left the ground, we flew.

Time made me soft around the edges, fog-throated,
an October patois, and though I betrayed you
I never was untrue.

Before you ask about the mercury and needles
understand, I'm talking about weather, how
the wind is always moving on
and snow becomes
salt, burning in my hands.

Your angels were faithless, lines of light dividing
air and dust. Transparent—you, the future,
most of all, your disappointment.

Before you ask what I mean by *disappointment*
understand, those were butter days,
of heat and sweet corn,
nights of loose horses running through us,
the shine of their silken knees.

Notes

The title *"What he kissed in me"* is from
Anne Marie Rooney's poem:
Last Evening: Index of first lines

The first line of "The Hazards of Magic" is
from Anne Marie Rooney's poem:
Last Evening: Index of first lines

About the Author

Susan Elbe is the author of *Eden in the Rearview Mirror* (Word Press) and a chapbook, *Light Made from Nothing* (Parallel Press). Her poems have appeared or are forthcoming in many literary journals, including *Ascent, Blackbird, Calyx, Crab Orchard Review, diode, Nimrod, North American Review, Prairie Schooner, Smartish Pace, Valparaiso Poetry Review* and on Verse Daily.

Susan also has work appearing or forthcoming in many anthologies, including *A Face to Meet the Faces: An Anthology of Contemporary Persona Poems*, eds. Oliver de la Paz and Stacey Lynn Brown (The University of Akron Press), *Fire On Her Tongue: An eBook Anthology of Contemporary Women's Poetry*, eds. Kelli Russell Agodon and Annette Spaulding-Convy, e-book, (Two Sylvias Press), *City of the Big Shoulders: An Anthology of Chicago Poems*, ed. Ryan Van Cleave (University of Iowa Press), and *A Fierce Brightness: Twenty-five Years of Women's Poetry* (Calyx Books).

Among her awards are the 2011 Concrete Wolf Chapbook Prize, the 7th Annual Oneiros Press Broadside Competition, The Poetry Center of Chicago's 14th Annual Juried Reading (third place), the CALYX inaugural Lois Cranston Memorial Poetry Prize, and the Council for Wisconsin Writers' Lorine Niedecker Award. She has received a Rowland Foundation residency to the Vermont Studio Center, a residency to the Virginia Center for Creative Arts, and two residencies to Edenfred in Madison, Wisconsin sponsored by the Terry Family Foundation. Susan has previously served on the

Council for Wisconsin Writers Board of Directors and on the Wisconsin Poet Laureate Commission. She and three other poets have collaborated with the Chazen Museum of Art in Madison, Wisconsin to present the Bridge Poetry Series, biennial readings showcasing ekphrastic poems based on a museum exhibition. You can learn more about her at www.susanelbe.com.

Also from Concrete Wolf Poetry Chapbook Series

A Broken Escalator Still Isn't the Stairs 2011
Chuck Carlise

Four of a Kind 2010
Mark Neely

Black Box Theater as Abandoned Zoo 2009
Dana Elkun

What Sound Does It Make 2008
Erin Malone

Eastlake Cleaners When Quality & Price Count [a romance] 2007
Janet Norman Knox

A Pilgrim's Guide To Chaos in the Heartland 2006
Jessica Goodfellow

Special Two Chapbook Issue 2005
Put Your Sorry Side Out & The Way Out West
Lois Marie Harrod and J.R. Thelin

Squeezers 2004
Alison Pelegrin

Such Short Supply 2003
Michelle Brooks

The Tallahassee Letters 2002
Ryan G. Van Cleave

The Grape Painter 2001
Lou Suarez

www.ingramcontent.com/pod-product-compliance
Lightning Source LLC
Chambersburg PA
CBHW022345040426
42449CB00006B/723